edited by Herman C. Ahrens, Jr.

PILGRIM PRESS   Philadelphia / Boston

TUNE IN

acknowledgments

Benson, John, pages 8, 28, 41
Brink, Frederick W., pages 17, 24–25, 33, 44, 58, 77
Fulton, Robert, pages 86–87
Kaufman, Anna, pages 13, 38, 52–53, 71
Knight, Christopher G., page 21
Morrisey, Carole, pages 1, 37, 69, 96
Musée d'Art et d'Histoire, Geneva, page 70
Schlaifer, Peter, page 48

foreword

My mail is full of surprises. Unusual requests. Bitter complaints. Songs of praise. I've-got-a-personal-problem confessions that bring tears to your heart. Literary outpourings that fill one's being with joy. You name it, we get it. And I try to answer each one responsibly.

But over the years there's been one persistent reaction and inquiry to which I've never been able to respond adequately— until now !

"The prayers in your magazine are real."

"Of all things in your magazine, the prayers are best."

"Have you ever considered printing a book of your best prayers ?"

That's why this collection of prayers from *Youth* magazine is being published — simply because enough of you have asked for it !

But why print prayers in *Youth* magazine at all ?

The teen years are life-shaping. As each of us breaks free of
childhood and dependency upon parents into adulthood and
making — and living with — our own decisions, we are helped most
by full acceptance as a human being, by standards against which
to test our own ideas, by a perspective of life that reveals its deeper
purpose, and by a hope that extends far beyond tomorrow. At
the heart of such a life-shaping environment is, we believe, personal
knowledge of and faith in God. Thus our sharing of prayers is one
way of affirming that God is alive, that our everyday lives are
closely tied to his intended way for this world, and that prayer
is a getting-to-know-God-and-his-way discipline which cannot
be learned too early.

These prayers were written by people to whom God is an honest
reality. These writers don't know you personally, but as you read
their prayers you will come to know a little more about them
and about their understanding of who God is, what life is all about,
and where each of us fits into the scheme of things. These prayers
were written by people of all ages. But if there is a feeling of
reality in these prayers, then the age of the writer is not important.
Genuineness knows no generation gap.

If God is for real, then a prayer is about real people, real problems,
real gropings, real dreams and joys, and for real occasions. If God

is love, then a prayer reflects an atmosphere of basic trust, an honesty unlimited, a giving of one's self to another — as well as a confidence of forgiveness and continued acceptance even if you fail or doubt for a moment.

If God is for all people, then a prayer is so personal that you feel it is your own, yet it is so universal that it is meaningful for others too. If God is the father of all creation, then a prayer is our best thinking about truth and the order of things. And it reflects an assurance that the way of a loving father for his children is good and ultimately victorious.

Each prayer is different. Each moment of meditation is different. Each person is different. But each prayer is an effort to tune in to what God and life and you and I are all about.

If in the privacy of your room or amid loneliness away from your loved ones, with a friend at a favorite place or with a group gathered for worship, at a time of joy or at a time of crisis, at a silent retreat high in the hills or along the beach of a crowded resort — if a single reader is helped to tune in, we will feel it has been worth it all.

— *Herman C. Ahrens, Jr.* **7**

preface

Dear God, do I have to talk to you in so-called religious language ?
Do I have to talk to you about "safe" subjects which won't offend
anyone ? Or can I get through the veneer with which we manage
to separate ourselves in the world, and talk about the things
that actually concern me ? Please let me talk that way, God, so
that I can be real to you, and not have to filter everything through
the strainer of religious and social appropriateness.

I know that I won't get many black and white answers when I talk
with you ; but I get the idea from past experience that you know
what it's like to live in the gray, and I guess that knowing you
know makes it easier to wrestle with things.

Be with me, God, as I share my thoughts with you. You have
promised to make me free. Grant that, as the first step toward that
complete freedom, I may be free in the way I talk to you. Amen.

— William W. Finlaw   **9**

world, i am youth

World, I am Youth, unsettled and searching,
Exploring the heights and the plain.
I wander your deserts, thirsty and pale,
I weep in the beating rain.
Ascend I the mountains with eagerness,
Hungry, and seeking my goal,
Then into barbs of stinging thorns
I fall with deluded soul.
In your shadows of dusk I tremble.
I fear death and even life.
Tomorrow I laugh, and confidence
Pervades my daily strife.
World, I am Youth, the hope of your day,
I'm bewildered and young in this land.
I'm searching your paths for a vision called truth
— Give me your hand.

— *Ellen Bryan*

life is a blast!

Life is a blast — my Lord !
A glorious dance pursued in delirious confusion.
Melodies and rhythms express the yearnings
    of our souls for the full-fledged drama of existence.
But when the music stops, when the driving beat is
    stilled, when the last partner leaves the floor,
We are so alone, so afraid, so bewildered.
For in the quiet and holy hours of our lives
We must face thee, and we are ashamed.
Ashamed of our coldness to our friends' need,
Ashamed of our blindness to the world's hunger,
Ashamed of our laziness when there's a creation to be fulfilled.
Transform the energies of our lives
    to thy creative purpose, and use us
    to the glory of all mankind.

— Andrew J. Young   **11**

we give thanks . . .

O give thanks to the Lord, for he is good.
We thank thee for hamburgers with onions,
    for french fries and cokes,
For thick, juicy steaks, for ice-cold milk,
For salted cashew nuts, for hot, buttered rolls.
For delicious apples, and milk cheddar cheese.

O give thanks to the Lord, for he is good.
We thank thee for madras plaid, and rough-textured tweeds,
For blue jeans, tennis shoes, and big, sloppy sweatshirts,
For cashmere sweaters, and Italian-made sandals,
For warm, wooly knee socks, and soft, roomy loafers.

O give thanks to the Lord, for he is good.
We thank thee for summer with its sun,
    its burning sand and sea.
For the crunching of autumn leaves underfoot
(Though we do not like to rake them).
For rainy days, with solitude and self-reflection,
And for Christmas trees and the spirit of giving.

O give thanks to the Lord, for he is good.
We give thanks for those "special"
     teachers, and for those who try, but still don't make it.
For a community that values education,
And for that rare moment when we find joy
     in learning for its own sake.
For good minds, inherited by the grace of God,
For being able to discover new books
     and exciting ideas,
And for Friday and the weekend.

O give thanks to the Lord, for he is good.
We thank thee for the color and excitement of football games,
And for the spirit and fun of pregame rallies.
For the freedom and self-expression in rock 'n' roll,
And for the butterflies of anticipation before that big dance.
For Friday nights at the "Y" and Saturday nights at the show,
And for our Sunday nights together, and our weekend trips to camp.

O give thanks to the Lord, for he is good.
We thank thee for the feeling that binds us to one
     another, though we're too embarrassed to call it love.

For the person who is close enough to understand us,
    accept us, and tell us what we're really like.
And for the person who offers his ear when we need
    to be heard.
We thank thee, Father, for our human parents, who mean
    well, and even do well, more than we would like
    to admit.

O give thanks to the Lord, for he is good.
We thank thee for the church which reminds us of
    thy claim upon our lives in spite of our own wishes
    to live unto ourselves.
For the wonder and awe of our own person and for the
    hope and promise of what we can become in you
    and with each other.
For what we can give to others and the world,
    in spite of our own secret inferiorities.
And above all, we thank thee for the love of Christ,
    and the clue of thy presence in this crazy, mixed-
    up, wonderful world.

— Karen Kromhout and E. Larry Beggs   **15**

love and you

may Your cool dear groovy girl style
turn me on to dear You   too

may the contoured symmetry
of her animated motionlessness
may the moistly mingled articulation of tongues
tenderly turning tumbling trembling
in intimate inquiry and invitation
in the wordless whispering
of this darkening quiet
turn us outward on to dear You   too

may we in playing   pray
in incredulous thanks and tingling joy
that such a crazy Word from You
could become in us
together
such terrific flesh

do You really love every us
as together we love each other !
her symmetry   dear You
and mine   You did form
just for this   didn't You !

and   O K   for more

out of some   or even most
of the crazy words You use
whose symmetry turned on Christ
the Only Man   even for girls
please form some serving symmetry
in the quivering ecstasy of our
celebrating Christ's resurrected
flesh
now
in each of grateful faithful us

— *Joseph Howell*

the gift of sex

O God,
I thank you for my sex.

I don't entirely understand it.
Sometimes I exult in it ; sometimes it tempts me,
    frightens me, torments me.
I want to claim it, to know when to command it
    and when to surrender it.

I have read the words of your Son —
How you made us, male and female, in your own image,
How man and wife become one flesh at your bidding.

I did not make my sex.
I did not decide to be boy or girl, man or woman.
I did not create the surging vitality within myself.
What I did not decide, I recognize and affirm.

Yet I do decide what my sex will mean to others and to me.
Scientists tell me that instinct controls sex in birds and beasts.
An animal breeder told me that there is no rape in the
    animal kingdom.
But men and women can use their sex according to their will.
They can meet each other in shared affection,
    or they can use and abuse themselves and each other.
Their sex may mean cruelty or tenderness,
        exploitation or fidelity, destruction or creativity.

O God, may my choices be genuine decisions, not caprices;
    affirmations, not defeat.

I see around me many possibilities.
I see mothers and fathers, bound together in love,
    creators and guardians, under God,
    of new lives.
I see a priest, who has made vows of chastity, whose
    masculine energies serve mankind. I see a nun,
    chaste, yet intensely feminine.
I see many who use their sex to tease and tantalize, to lure
    and punish, to compete, to sell the products of industry,
    to coax money from foolish spenders, to seek escape
    from their own anxieties.
I may choose, I must choose what my sex will be. O God,
    may my choices be genuine decisions.

A prophet once wrote, "All flesh shall see the salvation of God."
O Creator God, bless our human flesh.
May I appreciate its beauty in myself and others.
May I recognize my flesh, not simply as my possession,
    but as myself.
May I know your creative power, your saving power, in my flesh.

O God, I thank you for my sex.

— Roger L. Shinn   **19**

the marvel of a car

O God,
I thank thee for the marvel of a car — alive and powerful at the
touch of my hands and feet — a thing of tremendous
    possibilities — wonderful or terrible!
Help me to achieve the skill that will control it completely and
wisely, like a tool, shaping a better life for me and those
    around me.
I thank thee for the promise of adventure that is mine each time
I slip behind its wheel:
    the thrill of the open road . . . far places . . . strange sights . . .
    new "neighboring."
Make me aware, as I drive the streets of my town — signaling,
stopping, waiting, turning, and zooming ahead — that
I do not have to do merely with trucks, taxis, cars,
bicycles, and pedestrians, but with PEOPLE!
    People such as I know and touch as I walk the sidewalks
    and enter the homes of my neighborhood;
    people such as I am — making mistakes, perhaps, but not
    really wanting to.
Because I like people and know how important their happiness
and how precious they are to thee . . .
    Let me be alert, courteous, patient,
    considerate of the rights of others on the road,
    gracious enough to give up some rights of my own,
    and always . . . careful, realizing that:
        another's pain would destroy my pleasure,
        another's loss would rob my gain,
        and the life I save is just as precious as my own.
            Amen.

                    — Ernst H. Nussmann

the fun of sports

Lord, thank you for the fun and excitement of sports.
    For the energy and endurance of my body,
    For coordination and control,
    For patience and persistence,
    For opportunities to practice and train,
    For the help of coaches and friends,
                I am grateful, dear God.
Help me keep my work and learning and play in balance.
Show me in all athletic activities the values of
    keeping physically fit,
    working with others,
    striving for a goal,
    being honest at all costs,
    losing without shame,
    winning without pride.
May I use this body of mine to receive treasures of
forgiveness, peace, and eternal life.
        Amen.

— *Herman C. Ahrens, Jr.*

the pause

I saw an old man yesterday, God. He must have been ninety years old, all bent over and barely able to walk. But Lord, my heart didn't go out to him in love or even pity. Instead I felt a kind of revulsion. That scared me. What kind of a terrible person am I that I felt that way? I could at least have pitied him.

Could it be that I saw myself seventy-five years from now, and that it scared me a little? All the things that I count on to make me what I am, these can all be withered by age. My looks, my vitality, my health, my pleasing personality, my youth itself — these are all going to leave me someday. And then what will I be? Will I be an old person who can only attract pity, or worse, revulsion?

Maybe I need some deeper definition of myself, God. Maybe I need to do some searching as to what it is that really makes me, me. It's got to be more than the things I've listed, Lord, because they'll soon be gone. Please help me to know myself in a deeper way than I do now. Amen.

— *William W. Finlaw*   **23**

the blessed thespian

Here I am . . . on stage ;
    I love the applause, I glory in it.
    My mask smiles . . .
                I'm pretty.
    My face smiles momentarily . . .
              I'm ugly.
I play my roles quite convincingly —
    Lover . . .
         Christian . . .
             Musician . . .
  sincere . . .
        virtuous . . .
          talented . . . .
I'd even believe them myself
              if it weren't for intermission.

24

— *Jan Miller*

to belong and be free

Lord, I want to belong.
    Bill says, "Get a car."
    Fran tells me, "Win a letter."
    My dad says, "Study harder."
    John shouts, "Raise hell !"
    Kay asks, "Why not go steady ?"
I don't know which one is right.
All those things might work, I guess.
Still, each in its own way, Lord,
Is a trap.
And I choose to be free.

— Robert R. Hansel   **25**

how free are we, lord?

Lord, you say in Christ there is perfect freedom !

Turn right ! Turn left !
    Pressure — pressure — pressure.
    Where is the freedom, Lord ?

Which way ? What choice ?
    Decisions — decisions — decisions.
    Where is the freedom, Lord ?

What's right ? What's wrong ?
    Sort out — sort out — sort out.
    Who knows ? Who can help, Lord ?

Take parents, Lord !
    The din, din, din of don't, don't, don't . . . .
      Why won't they tell the straight story, Lord ?
      Why do they always beat around the bush, Lord ?
    The drive, drive, drive for marks, marks, marks . . . .
      Why do they push — so hard, so hard ?
    College, college, college — ya gotta, ya gotta,
                              ya gotta . . . .

Take the gang, Lord !
    Dress alike, smoke alike, dance alike . . .
    Follow, follow, follow the crowd . . . .
    Do, do what everybody else does . . . .
    Join, join, join the club — get lost, get lost . . . .

Turn right ! Turn left !
        Older generation — they don't understand.
        Tuned out, tuned out . . . .

Turn right ! Turn left !
        The bomb, the bomb.
        The world's going to end.
        Get everything out of life today . . . .

Turn right ! Turn left !
        Changes, changes — rapid changes.
        Confusion — pressure — confusion.
        Kids — parents — society — the bomb — no time !
        Grow up ! Grow up ! Quick, grow up fast !

Wait a minute !
        Lord, where am I ?
        Lord, when am I ?
        Lord, who am I ?
        Freedom to be ! ? Who, me ?

Lord, what a mess . . . .

Maybe the only thing that counts, Lord, is
        that somehow I know YOU understand.

                    Amen, Amen.

                            — *Peggy Morrison*   **27**

i told him how i felt

I tried to share something with my minister, Lord. I hung around after our young people's meeting, and asked if I could talk with him. I thought he would understand.

I told him how I felt, that I was so lonely, and sensed that none of the other kids really liked me. He told me that that just couldn't be true, how just the day before the president of our group had told him how much help I was. He said that I was making too big a thing out of the freeze I felt, that maybe the other kids just didn't feel like being friendly that night, that maybe they had problems, too, and I should try harder to understand them. He told me that if I would just stop and take a good, long look, I would find that I was as popular as any member of the group.

Lord, why wouldn't he believe me? Will you? Amen.

— *William W. Finlaw* **29**

lonely,
but never alone

I'm lonely sometimes, God, but I'm
    never alone . . . .
I'd like to have some privacy — but
    the world is always watching :
    through the eyes of family,
      or friends,
      or teachers,
      or even total strangers.
I need time to think and a chance to
    have thoughts and ideas that are
    mine alone — that don't have to
    be shared, or reported, or
    analyzed.
Lord, help me to be able to keep myself
    even while I share myself.
As society shapes me, may I still be
    able to be different — to be
    a person,
      TO BE —
For Christ's sake.
        Amen.

          — Laura-Jean Mashrick

one word

God,
words of advice like alphabet soup
spoon-fed at the family supper table
spill stale leftovers at my place
setting ;
words of usage in ancient capitals
repeated for modern world-history class
stall before question marks forty student heads
high.

I'm up to my ears in words, God,
words sticking to the roof of my mouth,
taped for now stored against when.

God.
(Repeat for unison.)
The Word
uni-versed fresh
in single-tongued flesh,
a word everyman can attest
if only in lowercase letters.   Amen.

— *Inez Long*   **31**

life is great, god!

Life is great, God.
My parents love me,
        even when they don't understand me.
My brothers are fun,
        even if they do tease.
I have plenty to eat,
        clothes to put on,
        a room of my own.
Friends !
I'm lucky and happy,
And want to thank you for all my blessings.

But . . .
I'm scared of the future.
As you have sustained me in the past,
Help me to trust you, and myself,
        during the days ahead.
                        Amen.

— *Laura-Jean Mashrick*

qualification

Uh . . . Lord ?
I wanted to thank you
For all you've given me.
I *wanted* to.
But see,
Really,
All I can do is
Ask *forgiveness*
That I can't sincerely thank you,
Lord,
For all that is mine.
You see —
As you know —
None of my possessions
Has ever been taken from me.

Of course,
I'm not indirectly asking
For adversity or
Deprivation.
Just forgiveness . . .
Know what I mean ?
That's all I want.

— Becky Schlemmer   **33**

don't you?

You aren't forgotten every day, Lord.
I remembered you
(Remember?)
Today when that kid
Ran in front of a car.
And yesterday,
When Mom was out late
And we worried.
And last week
When the neighbor's dog got sick.
Remember?
I inhaled:
    O God,
And exhaled:
    Help him,
    Help her,
    Help it.

See? I don't forget you every day.
Just remember when I . . .
You *do* remember today,
                    yesterday,
                    last week,
When I . . .
Don't you?!

34   — *Becky Schlemmer*

the rich
young man scares me

I am scared by the story of the young man
who met the Christ himself
and yet turned his back and walked away.

His "riches" were too much for him.
He closed his eyes to the needs of others,
and shut out the Master
who could have given him true greatness.

I am scared because my eyes want to close, too.
The one who turned his back lives very near,
while He seems far away.

Lord of Life,
fill my conscience full of thy spirit of love.
Occupy my mind. Subdue my selfishness.

Grant me, dear God,
the strength to face with firmness
my brother and my Master,
that what I am and have will serve thy will,
and all my walking will be on the path
of his divine steps.

Amen.

—*James O. Gilliom*   **35**

jonah and me

As you speak to me, O God,
I see the need in Nineveh.
But I refuse to go.
Those people are not worth saving.

> I see the lonely pass me
> in the halls at school, but who
> wants to be the friend of an outcast?

> I see sad, scrawny faces
> in photos from overseas.
> Thank God, I'm in America.

Leave me alone, God!
Must you follow me everywhere?
Why don't you punish those evil people
in Nineveh and be done with it?
Why must I suffer for their sins?

> Why does that ugly guy always
> get assigned to the same
> classroom as mine?

> Why do those ungrateful Asians
> and Africans condemn our
> peace-loving nation?

Here I am, Lord. I have preached
your prophecy of doom.
But look what's happening!
These people listen and repent!
I just can't understand how
you can forgive such sinners!

> That oddball is now class prexy.
> And he gave me a top committee
>   post!
> He's really weird!

> Those young nations want
> to become democracies, too!
> Their people die for freedom!
> What's the world coming to?

And now, Father, you are even
willing to forgive me!

— *Herman C. Ahrens, Jr.*

i

The tight shell of me,
The cool enclosure of I,
The selfishness of myself.
The personal desire,
The singular pleasure,
The sole purpose,
The only want :
The inferior you,
The superior me.

Break loose, my spirit,
And be free.

38   *— Lonn Wolf*

you are my friend

It just occurred to me, God, that I don't have a real friend. I've
been thinking over all my acquaintances, and there's nobody on my
list who can qualify. There are lots of people I like, and who
I think like me, but I have the feeling that that's about as deep
as it goes.

Whom can I trust, Lord, to let him see me as I really am? I've always
got to play little games. Show a little, see how it's handled,
before I dare show any more. But there is no one with whom
I can go deeper than the first few "showings." They either tell me
I shouldn't feel that way, or try to explain my feelings away, or
pull away themselves as though my reality frightens them. I know
that I'm not perfect. And I want honest criticism from people
I respect. Even so, can't people just accept me for what I am?
Am I some sort of kook, Lord, because I want to be friends, and
because I feel that being friends means that I can be me?
Can't friends communicate person to person honestly instead
of spending all their time playing games with trivia?

God, maybe if you will be my friend, then I can take it from there.
Will you let me go beyond the first showings, down to where
I really want to and need to communicate? Will you simply accept
my feelings for what they are, and never pull away? I guess
that I will have to believe that you will.

Thank you, God, simply for wanting to be my friend.   Amen.

— William W. Finlaw   **39**

a bridge across

I need a bridge, Lord, across the chasm
    separating me
        from the rest of the human race;
A bridge to span the space between
    the darkness of loneliness
        and the light of belonging.

Life's crammed with feelings and ideas
    that need sharing,
        ideas that would tell the world I exist, I am real.
But I am dumb. I cannot speak for fear
    of being discovered;
        for fear that someone might expect too much of me.

What's wrong, Lord? Are others afraid
    and lonely too,
        silenced by their own self-centered nothingness?
Do other people need a bridge as desperately as I?
    Has that anything to do
        with why you sent a Savior?

— *Nancy Ross*

on the collect for purity

Almighty God, unto whom all hearts are open, all
desires known, and from whom no secrets are hid . . .

Here we are, God ;
  We are tall and short,
  We are lean and large.

Here we are, God ;
  Some of us are shook up,
  Some of us are loose,
  Some of us don't even know.

Here we are, God ;
  We think we want to be useful,
  But we feel like we're only being used.
  We even want to be faithful,
  But we can't find anything to believe.

Here we are, God ;
  Don't let anybody know we're afraid ;
  Don't tell anyone that we have no hope.

We're sorry your Son got killed.
They tell us this was a good thing,
But to us it just seems that nice guys
    finish last.

Here we are, God;
    We are all we've got,
    But we don't know what we've got.
    We are here to begin,
    But we don't know what we're beginning.
    It's hard to pray and worse to think.
    God, are you ever confused?
    God, do things ever bug you?

Tell us, God, because here we are.

. . . Cleanse the thoughts of our hearts by the inspiration of thy Holy Spirit, that we may perfectly love thee and worthily magnify thy holy name; through Christ, our Lord.   Amen.

— John McAllister   **43**

the desert

God, people talk about periods of spiritual dryness. They say
that if I can't feel your nearness sometimes, to keep working at it;
that the dryness will pass if I don't give up.

Do you want to know something, Lord? I can't ever remember
a period of "wetness." I mean, as hard as I have tried, I never get
the feeling that is supposed to come to me. Am I hopeless?
Are you really there listening? Please let me feel your presence
just once, so I'll know what it's like.

Do you think, God, that I can go on by simply believing with
all my heart that you do hear; that it doesn't make any difference,
in terms of your listening, if I feel it or not.

I'll try it that way, Lord, but you sure aren't making it easy
on me.   Amen.

— William W. Finlaw   **45**

how do i pray
when i don't know
where to turn

Sometimes I feel so mixed up,
I don't know where to turn.

My problems seem so big and complex
that no solutions seem right or adequate.
I grope for answers that aren't there
until I wonder if something's wrong with me.
If friends and family knew my torment,
would they laugh at my weakness?

The world overwhelms me.
    I'm confused.
My mind lacks answers.
    I'm afraid.
There's nobody to turn to.
    I'm lonely.
My thoughts are of me alone.
    I'm selfish.

Who can help me rise above it all,
if only for a moment,
    to see some order amid confusion,
    to glimpse truth amid the unknown,
    to have confidence amid fear,

to envision purpose amid emptiness,
to give instead of get,
to know love that never fails?

I want to get outside myself,
not to escape, but to see life
in a perspective that is bigger than I.
I do not seek easy answers,
but right answers.
I doubt and question,
but this is part of my searching.
I want to be loved
For what I am and do.

O God, who has formed life and knows all,
who seeks to save us from aimlessness and sin,
who loves us always,
Help me to trust thee as Father and Friend,
to unload my problems in thy presence,
to seek right answers in the light of thy will,
to give of myself in service to thee and others.

O God, help me to pray.

— Herman C. Ahrens, Jr.   **47**

the thirst

O God, help me to pray.
Quiet my restlessness and
still my noisy desires.
Turn me toward your deep
wells and away from my own
shallow waters. Center me
down into your love. Force
me to let you hold me tightly.

O God, push me to dare to
live on tiptoe. Stop me
from being suspicious of
enthusiasm or happiness or
friendship. Lead me toward
knowing another by giving
of myself. Guide me
toward loving leaps of faith.

O God, mold me with the clays
of forgiveness and hold me
in the hands of love. Draw
me into the wells of
your joy. Show me how to
drink of deep waters. And
help me, O God, to admit how
thirsty I really am.
                Amen.

— *Joan Hemenway*

here we are
through lent

Here we are through Lent, God.
It's Easter . . .
    but that's not how I act.
I act as if —
    "Well, that's over for another year!"

God, help me to rejoice and be glad;
To feel the reality and wonder of the
    resurrection
  with my whole being;
To be able to mean "Hallelujah!"
    as I mean my shouts of joy
    when I discover a truth and
     really understand it,
    when someone cares,
    when work I've done is
     praised and appreciated.
May the reality of Easter awaken this
    depth of feeling and meaning
     in all my life,
    so I can look at life —
    and death —
    and shout
    "Hooray!"

— Laura-Jean Mashrick **49**

easter

A great earthquake shakes a stone loose from a tomb.
It is bare, the robes are empty,
And Mary cries out in fear.

The night is dark and lonely and the day long and flat.
A life is numb ; a heart is empty.
I cry out in fear.

O God, where is my center, my soul, my being ?
O God, my God, why hast thou forsaken me ?

And the disciples went to a mountain in Galilee.
They worshiped and were commanded
To go,
To teach,
To know . . .
      for lo, I am with you always, to the close of the age.

And fear and trembling shook the earth with joy.

50
—Joan Hemenway

guided in silence
by a loving hand

Alone and in silence I watch the placid lake.
Deceptive water . . . now tranquil, now turbulent,
Like life in its make.

Alone and in silence I meet each dawning day.
Confusing hours . . . now joyful, now sorrowful.
What do these contrasts say ?

O God, alone and in silence let me not be.
Now tranquil, now turbulent, now laughing, now
    suffering
Alone . . . life asks too much of me.

But guided in silence by thy loving hand
In all of life . . . now peaceful, now struggling . . .
Unafraid I can stand.   Amen.

— Kay Lorans Hancock   **51**

swing to the rhythm of life!

Music is me, man !

I dance ! I prance !
I jazz with joy !
I woo ! I worship !
I chorus my praise !

I want to swing and beat
with the rhythm of life.
I want to shout ! Weep !
Feel the mood of the moment !
I want to blend into one
As each finds harmony.

Music is art, man !

A myriad of colors . . .
The full scale of life . . .
Not one touch the same,
Yet known to all men.

Music is you, God.

— *Herman C. Ahrens, Jr.*   **53**

help me to speak out

God, I want to speak out,
    To be free to express myself
        in words, or paint, or music.
But I can't!
Oh, I'm physically free —
    But emotionally tied up.
Help me, Lord, to be able to speak,
    To be honest and open about myself and my world,
    To not be afraid that someone may laugh — or cry.
O God, through thy love may I be free also to love;
    And therefore free
        to speak,
           or paint,
             or sing,
               or write,
                  or dance.
                    Amen.

— *Laura-Jean Mashrick*

how can i know
the other guy's pain?

Almighty God,

I, who have never known what it means not to have the things
I desire, need to *feel* the poverty and hunger and despair among
my fellowmen.

I, who have felt nothing but the surge of youthful vitality in my
body, need to *understand* what it means to be ill and unable to
care for myself.

I, who have never stood alone in the crowd as odd or unacceptable,
need to *sense* what it means to be judged and rejected by the
color of my skin.

I, who have never experienced the desperation of a dependence
on drug or drink, need to *realize* the hell of an addiction
I cannot escape.

I, who have never really suffered or sacrificed or died, pray that
I may become painfully aware of my brother's great need and that
I may *ache* until I have reached out with honest help.

— Kay Lorans Hancock   **55**

worlds in conflict

My worlds are in conflict, O God.
I laugh at life's absurdities, but I'm told I lack respect for life.
I want to be beautiful in body and being,
    but some call your gift of sex sinful and some scoff at virtue.
I volunteer to serve people who can't afford help,
    but I'm told not to do anything for anyone unless I get paid.
I'm condemned for demonstrating against community injustice,
    but brutality and mob rule are condoned by indifference.
I'm educated in a fast-changing, science-dominated world of
      the Bomb,
    but I'm asked to live and think as they did in past generations.
Some call this conflict rebellion or impatience,
Some call it controversy or subversion or revolution,
Some call it a search for truth —
    the edge of a breakthrough to new worlds.
Through the haze of this confusion and conflict,
Help me to know your truth for our world.

— *Herman C. Ahrens, Jr.*

the battered christ

His face was shattered

> **Man is empty, O God!**
> **We are afraid, suspicious, lonely,**
> **selfish, hateful, confused . . . .**

His clothes were torn

> **How do we fill the void, O God?**
> **Do we build walls, shout threats,**
> **gossip lies, exploit the innocent,**
> **starve the hungry, slap the unlovely . . . ?**

His body was battered

> **O God, we reach for a better way.**
> **Fill us with thy love.**
> **Nurture us in thy truth.**
> **Direct us in thy purpose.**

And truth was born!

— Herman C. Ahrens, Jr.   **57**

a longing for beauty

O GOD, WE HEAR VOICES OF UGLINESS AROUND US.

To hell with nigras ! If the good Lord wanted us to be brothers, he would have made us all one color ! / Kids got money to burn. Sell them something they don't need. They won't know any better. Cash in while they're green teens. It's good business. / What's wrong with cheating ? Everybody does it. Just don't let yourself get caught. / I hate my parents ! They treat me like a child, and yet they want me to act grown-up ! / He's a brain. He knows too much. Give him the cool treatment. That'll learn him ! / What a sucker ! He's got real talent. But he's wasting it on a church job. / Man, is she stacked ! That's my speed. Wait till I get her out on a date. / They oughta fire that old man. He's over fifty — way past his prime. Don't be sentimental, be efficient. / That's no religious painting. I can't figure it out. It bothers me. These modern artists are all mixed up. / Being Catholic is bad enough. But did he have to marry a Puerto Rican ?

IN THE MIDST OF THIS UGLINESS, O GOD,
HELP US TO KNOW BEAUTY.

— Herman C. Ahrens, Jr. **59**

a psalm of spring

O God,
The sun pours down on the earth, on the lovely land
that you have given us to enjoy.
    I am filled with hope.
The breeze that sings of spring makes me want to laugh, to cry,
to walk tall, to shout to the world that I am young and free.
    I am filled with joy.
The warmth that fills the air makes me yearn to touch another,
to love another, to do things for another, to give of myself,
to truly live.
    I am filled with desire.
The seeds of spring are in me, O God.
The seeds of spring *are* me, O God. Help me to nurture their
special needs. Help me to grow into completeness of being.
Let my hope, my joy, my desire be expressed in ways
that are beautiful to you and to me.
    I am filled with thanks.

— *Kay Lorans Hancock*

what about tomorrow?

What does the future hold?

This bothers me sometimes, God.
But it's exciting too.
The possibilities for good and bad
        both seem infinite.

I would thank you, God, for this creation —
        for the fact that I'm here
        in the midst of it,
        whatever happens.
Help me to remember that you are the
        creator and giver of all gifts.
And as each day passes, as the future
        races into the present,
May I see you in the future as in the past;
May I — in faith and hope — act, work,
        and live
To help things happen, not just wait
        for them.   Amen.

— *Laura-Jean Mashrick*   **61**

we stand in awe

How wonderful is your creation, O God!
We stand in awe before
    The vastness of the universe,
       whose magnitude and wonder
       grow in men's minds with
       every new scientific insight.
    The miracle of man,
       whose staggering achievements
       are but the meager scratchings
       of the fullest potential
       you intended for him.
    The mystery of creation itself,
       which causes men to ask:
       "How did it all start?
       Why are we here?"
    The orderliness of life,
       as seen in the natural laws
       governing atoms and humans,
       the remotest stars and the
       smallest blades of grass.
    The unity of spirit,
       which we cannot always prove
       with facts, but which we often
       can feel with faith
       and unshakable certainty.
Keep us sensitive to the needs
of others. Help us to know your
will for us and for all creation.
Guide us, our Father.   Amen.

                      — *Herman C. Ahrens, Jr.*

science tells us much
but we know so little

We are staggered by what we find
    in our test tubes, our telescopes, our formulae —
    all creation unfolds before our mind.

But our hearts hurt.
    The smallest atom threatens us.
    The cure of disease is not shared.
    Easy living softens us.
    Life on other planets has us scared.
Are our souls too small to match the feats of our minds?
What is the purpose of it all?
What are we missing?

O God, forgive us when we forget
    that we are not the Creator, but the created ones;
    that we are not the Maker, but the users;
    that we are not the Father, but the children.

Creator God,
    How did you intend for all this to be?
Giver of all gifts,
    Help us to know how to use what you have given.
Beloved Father,
    Teach us to live your way of love.

— Herman C. Ahrens, Jr. **63**

is this your doing, lord?

We sing a song "the times they are a-changing."
And that's your doing, right, Lord?

Behind the blinking bank of lights that sends up the astronaut
    and runs the plant without people,
In laser beam that cuts both sore and steel,
Through electron path that soothes the feverish brain
    and beats the artificial heart,
    We see your skill.

Could it be that you are giving us a glimpse of a Great Vision
In which men no longer work by sweat of brow,
    but let the music in them sing;
When tears shall be wiped from eyes and
    "there shall be no more pain"?

    Yes, the times are changing.
64   The trouble is, we're not.

Lord, we take your computers and use them to make bigger bombs.
Christ, we let millions starve when we could
    make the deserts bloom.
Lord, we are tempted to turn men into robots with our tinkering.

Where will it all end?

Lord, we do not intend to let it end with bang or whimper.
We'll fight to see your gifts used for man,
And for the beauty of the earth as well.

In that task we'll not be alone.
You'll be alongside with grace
And out ahead with hope.

Blessing and honor, glory and power be to you!
Amen.

— Gabriel Fackre   **65**

in your hands we lay the world

Father,
    In your hands
      we lay the giants of this world ;
    In your hands
      we lay the black and the white,
        the rich and the poor,
        the young and the old ;
    In your hands
      we lay India and Pakistan,
        North and South Vietnam,
        Egypt and Israel,
        America and Russia ;
    In your hands
      we lay China,
        all the nations that try to develop,
        and all the nations that are developed.
All the gaps — we lay in your hands.

    Help us
      to build bridges and not widen the distances any further,
      to demask giants and not blow them up any bigger,

to look realities in the face
    and not shut them out from confrontation.

Help us
    to choose between the right and the wrong things to do;
        between going along with or being opposed to
        what our government, our society, our community, our
        schools are doing;
    to choose between the draft and conscientious objection;
    to participate critically and be real salt
        instead of sugar.

Enlighten our minds,
Give us vision,
Make us creative.
Help us struggle
    for the sake of the world, your world,
    the one world you promised us,
Our Father, who art in heaven.

— Annemarth van Lelyfeld   **67**

time

Time, where have you gone?
Time, why don't you go?
It is either/or,
But never both.

Sometimes time is light
And flies swiftly away,
With hardly a backward glance
Or departing whisper.

Sometimes it is so heavy
It thuds out each second,
Walking more and more slowly
Until it needs a push.

Which is it to be for me?
Is time to rule in seconds,
Or in years,
Or merely in silence?

Is time to mean a stopwatch,
Or a church-bell chime,
Or a toast
On New Year's Eve?

No. It is all these,
But it is also more.
Time is that which is to be filled
To the brim without overflowing.

Time is the great gift:
The hope of the future,
The love of the past,
The engagement of the present.

Time is possibility,
Endlessly.

—*Joan Hemenway*

money

O Father, grant us a proper attitude toward money. Thou hast
taught us that life does not consist of the abundance of things
that a person possesses. Save us from thinking that money is ever
an adequate measure of success. Forgive us for the moments
when we have coveted more of this world's goods than we really
need. Help us to look upon the money that we earn or that has
been given to us not as an end in itself, but as a means of doing
good. May we learn, as the apostle Paul did, how to be abased
and how to abound. Reveal to us, as thou didst to him, the secret
of facing plenty and hunger, abundance and want. Keep in our
remembrance at all times that it is by thy grace that we love
and prosper.   Amen.

— *Paul E. Strauch*

humor

Dear God, we are thankful for the gift of humor in everyday life.
    Amid sorrow and sour faces,
        we welcome moments of joy and sweetness.
    Amid our struttings of pride,
        we are embarrassed by the banana peels of humility.
    Amid the many tensions of the unknown,
        we are relieved by the gentleness of quiet laughter.
    Amid the tragedy of falseness and hate,
        we search for the comedy of truth and love.
    Amid our frequent wanderings from your way,
        we await the call to do your will.
                                        Amen.

— Herman C. Ahrens, Jr.   **71**

when school is a bore

It's the same old thing day after day. Listening to lectures.
Memorizing dates and data and formulae. No learning to think
things through. Always crummy kids. No talking with teachers as
friend to friend. Dissecting "literature" from the long-dead past.
Studying science outdated by this morning's headlines. Training
for a vocation soon to be doomed by automation. Cramming for
exams. Others cheat, while I sweat ! And always my parents
pushing me when I want to be free, and then not caring when
I need them most.

SOMETIMES I GET FED UP WITH SCHOOL !

O God, help me to rise above the temptations of the moment and
to see the bigger purpose which the present often hides.

I want to be grown-up, but I'm still growing. I want to do what's
right, but I'm not yet sure of right and wrong. I want to be accepted
for what I am, but who am I ? I need to know so much more before
the fullness of life is mine. Is not school my time for getting ready ?
O God, help me to make the most of it.

From the daily routine at school, help me to find a pattern of life.

From my mixing with all types of people, help me to grow in
understanding of myself and human nature.

From hours of study and lecture, help me to learn the disciplines of creative listening and informed thinking in my endless search for truth.

From men of ages past and events in the headlines today, help me to grasp a concept of humanity that will shape my perspective for facing the future.

From the maze of activities and assignments, help me to mold a mature sense of responsibility.

From the hypocrisy and confusion of today, help me to sift right from wrong and gain confidence in the right.

From the fast pace of today's living, help me to equip myself to meet the challenge of change, to find security in that which does not change, and to avoid being blindly swept along with the crowd.

From my "teachers" at home, at school, at church, and in the community, help me to firm a foundation for a life fitting to be called Christian.

— Herman C. Ahrens, Jr.   **73**

on being a student

Make me uncomfortable, O God.

Make me uncomfortable about what I'm doing with the mind
you have given me . . . about studying too little and too
sloppily . . . about memorizing facts rather than seeking truth
and knowledge . . . about working for grades rather than
for the excitement of learning.
Make me uncomfortable about my future hopes . . . about wanting
college as a means toward gaining a better-paying job,
more security, and social prestige rather than toward fulfilling
your highest purpose for me.

Disturb me, O God.

Until I sense that my true calling as a student is :
To grow into the broadest, deepest, most vital person possible ;
To seize now this awesome opportunity for searching out
wisdom ;
To find joy in reading and grappling and grasping ;
To live richly and responsibly ;
To do my part to help create a better world ;
To be constantly grateful for the capacity, creativity, and
courage that are given to me . . . freely . . . by thee.   Amen.

— *Kay Lorans Hancock*

summer is a time for growing

O God, help me not to waste this summer day.
Help me to remember that relaxation is good, but
not all that counts. Help me to use summer's
freedom for discovering talents in myself that I've
been too busy to notice before . . .
> for developing gifts that have too long lain idle . . .
> for doing work that is helpful to others and
>   educational for me . . .
> for reading books that enable me to grow in
>   knowledge and understanding . . .
> for sharing hours with friends in creative projects
>   as well as in idle fun.

Through casual leisure and constructive labor, stir
all that lies latent in me . . . till each new day
becomes a living thanks to thee.   Amen.

— Kay Lorans Hancock   **75**

no problems today,
just ''thank you''

Just this once, O God, I'd like to come to you with no problems,
but simply to say,
       ''Thank you . . .''
For your forgiveness, when I fail ;
For the sheer joy of sleep, when I'm terribly tired ;
For the silent strength of humility, when pride overtakes me ;
For the justice of your law, when men are cruel ;
For the growing remedies to good health, when I am ill ;
For the nurture of new knowledge, when I make a mistake ;
For the simplicity of orderliness, when I face confusion ;
For the joy of helping others, when I see people in need ;
For the assurance that you have made a place for each of us,
       when I feel inadequate among my peers ;
For the earthly evidences of your will, when I'm trying to
       find out what life is all about ;
For the reality of your world, when I stray too far into fantasy ;
For the rightness of reasonableness, when I panic too quickly ;
For the fun that refreshes, when everything gets too serious ;
For the renewal in moments of silence, when I'm dizzy being busy
       in a go-go world ;
For the confidence of friends, when my parents don't understand ;
For the healing love of family, when friends hurt me ;
For your presence, when I am very lonely.
And above all, God, I am thankful for the worthwhileness and
       fullness you have given to this world of yours.   Amen.

— *Herman C. Ahrens, Jr.*

our place in the family of man

Almighty God, you have given us the world and all that is therein.
Help us to care.
You have confronted us with hunger, poverty, illiteracy, disease,
    and ignorance.
Help us to be aware.
You have endowed us with intelligence, ingenuity, energies,
    resources, and skills.
Help us to share.
Help us to become increasingly sensitive to the needs
    of all your people everywhere.
Help us to work together to gain a better understanding
    of our place in the family of man.
Our lives will be our thanks.   Amen.

— Kay Lorans Hancock   **77**

a litany for racial justice

Leader : O Lord, Father and Protector of us all,
Thou who made us brothers and joined all hands
with the common link of love :

Youth : Search us, O God, and know our hearts ; try us and
know our thoughts.

Leader : Father, we have strayed from thy precepts ;
We have sinned against our brothers :
By withdrawal from their presence,
By ignorance and neglect of their human needs,
By absence of warmth and friendship,
By silence in the midst of wrong,
By empty promises too long postponed.

Youth : If we say we have no sin, we deceive ourselves.

Leader : We are not guiltless of the insult of separation and
the crime of injustice.
Upon our Pilate-hands are the tears and the blood
of our brother's desperation.
On our consciences is the despair of the deprived :
The thirsty who cannot drink,
The hungry who cannot eat,

The weary who cannot rest,
The disfranchised confined outside the gates of
 opportunity,
The shackled, the crippled, the disenchanted, the
 slain.

Youth : Wilt thou not revive us again ? Show us thy mercy,
 O Lord, and grant us thy salvation.

Leader : Help us to tear down the barriers that divide us
 from our neighbors :
Clear our cluttered gardens with the sunlight of thy
 love,
Uproot the stubborn weeds of intolerance and
 bigotry from the sandy clay of indifference,
Cover the ground with the fertile soil of goodwill,
And plant the seeds of unity and justice there.
Fortify us, commit us to thy righteousness.

Youth : Show us thy ways, O Lord ; teach us thy paths ; lead
 us in thy truth ; and restore us to thy joy forever.
 Amen.

— Nicholas Hood **79**

i love my country, but . . .

O God, I love my country. But my pride does not hide my discontent.
We have too easily forgotten that your love and truth molded the men
who shaped our nation's ideals of freedom, justice, and equality.

While we condemn the atheist enemy who denies you, many of us
ignore you.

While we grow fat with the luxury living of our prosperous
economy, we cringe at the pleas of poverty.

While we shout our slogans of freedom and equality, we push
aside minorities, we silence the voices of honest dissent, and
we nurture our own deep-rooted prejudices.

While we design computers to decipher our complex, fast-changing,
scientific world, we are soothed by easy answers.

While we boast of a country governed by the people, we are
stifled by the apathy of its good citizens.

O God, help me to know what is right. Nourish the love within me
that I may extend my hand to those who disturb me most.

— Herman C. Ahrens, Jr.

a youth's petition

Hear me, dear God, my plea rings out to thee.
My world this day knows not of love and peace.
It speaks of death and war and hate to me;
Its piercing screams are hell, O let them cease!
Its people arm with bow and gleaming spear.
They aim their lethal arrows skillfully;
They pull the string of life so taut, I fear
'Twill break and hell will reign eternally!

We must have peace, no other can succeed;
For life, all life, is close to death, and life
Itself is now just time and fear.   O lead
Us forward out of fear of bomb and knife;
Let peace of mind and world be thy great trust
To man; for war will take all life to dust!

— *David Hummon*   **81**

where is hope?

O God, where is there hope! Chaos, confusion, dislocation, hatred, greed, bloodshed, disobedience all about aplenty — but hope seems strangely lacking.

In every generation hope is one of the first casualties, and is recovered only as men learn to hope in you.

Speak to us the truth we need to hear: truth concerning the strength of goodness, the power of goodwill, your purpose in the world, and the steadfastness of those who trust in you.

We do not believe that the world is out of your hands. We do believe that, in spite of all that looks to the contrary, your purpose will be worked out. We would be a part of the process by which the world becomes the Kingdom. Help us in all this to hope in your unending love.

In spite of all, we hold fast to hope. Help us to love those who set themselves against what we believe is your purpose. Help us to keep from our own spirits the hatred that is so much a part of the world.

We pray and rely upon your steadfastness.   Amen.

— *Ben M. Herbster*

toward
a proliferation of human love

O God, we are tired of being compelled to hate in megatons and
to love according to Robert's Rules of Order. We are tired
of conventional goodness in an unconventional world.

Our weapons have proliferated, but not our love. We have rejected
unconditional love as a softening influence — a threat to
religious morality and to the American way of life. And for all love
that is not directed toward the "right" people in the "right "way
we have a word : illicit.

O God, for whom no genuine love is illicit, have mercy upon us
for being so timid about the one thing that matters ; and teach us
again how to rejoice with one another freely and without caution.
In the face of old and new hatreds in the world, give us courage
to love on a grander scale than ever — in cinemascope and
living color ! Grant us the experience we need and fear most :
a full epidemic of human, warm-bodied love.

In the name of the Christ whose passion for the world was
complete and unrestrained, we pray.

Amen.

— William T. Joyner   83

midwinter musings

In these twilight winter days,
Burrowed in dark evenings
And lanced by bright
    mornings,
We cringe in our futile
    attempts
To be more than human.

We try to catch today's train
With yesterday's timetable,
Or open the front door
With the back-door key.
We want to be in with our
    friends,
But not let our friends in.
We are freed by our hopes,
But caught in our disappoint-
    ments.

O God, when I cry to thee
How dost thou know my hurts,
My loneliness, my soul-
    burning?
There's just me here,
And the pillow,
And that train I missed,
And a bent, back-door key
Buried in the cold evening.
That's all, O God.
That's all
— I think.
Except the bright morning
To greet a twilight winter day.

—Joan Hemenway

when digging into the past

Out of the dark past,
symbols on an ancient boundary marker
remind us that we are not alone,
and that time has no boundaries.

      The very earth we walk on
      buries the debris of those who fathered us.
      We dig into the past and find —

The commonness of daily survival for all men . . .
The search for truth that threads through the ages . . .
The expression of a beauty that never fades . . .
The awe of worlds yet unknown . . . .

      And we wonder what our children's children
      in their new world of tomorrow
      will find when they prod among our ruins —

In the dust, the shards of shattered tubes . . .
In the streets, the telltale bones of a hopeless flight . . .
On the altars, embroidered tapestry and tarnished gold . . .
In a cave, the forgotten scrolls of holy writ . . .

      And in the night, the light of a lonely star.

— Herman C. Ahrens, Jr.   **85**

thanks for
muddy shoes

O God, we give thee thanks for
   muddy shoes
     which walk through your
     creation and rejoice,
   renewed bodies
     which breathe fresh air
     and become whole,
   wandering minds
     which are readied for the
     mysterious deeps of faith,
   anxious hearts
     which are opened to ourselves
     and to others and to you,
   churning souls
     which are calmed and cleansed
      and set on fire,
   lonely moments
     which hollow us out
     to be filled again,
   reconciled friendships
     which sustain us and
     restore us and heal,
   special times
     in which we share,
     together risking your love.
         Amen.

—Joan Hemenway

a prayer at graduation

Our Father God, we come to thee at a memorable moment in the
life of all men. We look upon a world which seems unlimited
in opportunity and self-satisfaction. Seated on the summit
of worldly achievement, we are tempted to pray, "O Man,
what is *God*, that thou art mindful of him?" May such a prayer
never be more than the youthful impatience of a growing mind.

Grant unto us who are sons of men the grace to become sons
of God. In our search for truth and the fullness of living, confront
us with *responsibility* rather than self-interest. Imbue us with
a discontent of that indulgence which draws a tight circle
around self.

*Where we would launch rockets, let them be missiles of service
rather than vainglory.*

*Where we would be physicians, let us be statesmen of medicine
who track the dark killers of man by the brilliant light of thy science.*

*Where we would be teachers and thinkers and writers, let us be
servants of integrity who grapple with the forces of injustice,
separation, and human folly.*

Silently, unknown to some and known to others, help us to be
the prophets and leaders of thy reign. May something of what
our school has taught us be used by thee to replace ignorance
with truth, and meaninglessness with purpose and power.
By thy grace we pray.   Amen.

— Richard E. Wentz   **87**

help me keep
my dreams alive

In a world of conflict and confusion,
Help me to keep my dreams alive, O God.

I dream of good health.
> Help me to be a worthy steward of the body which
> you have given me. May I never let my health suffer
> from personal neglect or injurious excess.

I dream of always being liked.
> Help me to be a true friend. And no matter how
> lonely I become when I'm away from home, never
> let me cast aside lifelong standards in exchange for
> shallow acceptance.

I dream of a happy home.
> Help me to see what it takes to be a good parent.
> May I never let silly infatuation, physical appearances,
> or momentary pleasure blur my understanding
> of that kind of love for a person that grows and
> lasts for a lifetime.

I dream of success in a job.
Help me to have confidence in my abilities, but also
to know my limitations. May success never be mine
if it is achieved by exploiting others.

I dream of right winning over wrong.
In the fight for justice and truth, help me to know
what's right. When I am wrong, help me to be big
enough to admit my error. When I am right, help
me to know how best to change what's wrong.

I dream of a world at peace.
Help me always to be deeply sensitive to the humanness
of my fellowman. When I am hungry, rejected,
sick, uninformed, poor, or treated as less
than human, it is hard for me, too, to live in harmony
with others.

O God, help me keep my dreams alive.

— Herman C. Ahrens, Jr.   **89**

o god, whose purpose
spans the ages

O God, whose purpose spans the ages,
    teach me thy will for the fleeting years that are mine.
May I spend them without sloth and without haste,
    buying up the whole value of every hour.
From this brief miracle of time grant me to fashion a life
    so strong with integrity,
    so rich in usefulness,
    so keen in understanding,
That it may stand up in the judgment
    to which death brings us all at last.
Eternal Spirit,
Whose power holds the galaxies of the sky,
    the ends of the earth,
    and the souls of all men
    within an invisible net of love,
Use me in thy mighty working.
Stretch me for a far-reaching vocation.
Toughen and strengthen me for whatever difficulty
    or pain my service may entail.
In a great and dangerous age, help me to live worthy
    of my generation,
    of my church,
    and of my Lord.
Amen.

— David Stowe

the prayer within the prayer

Our Father

Many of us think critically of the heritage of our fathers. Many
of us leave our homes because we do not understand our parents.
The world of our parents is so different from ours. You understand our troubles and hopes ; you accept our world without
haughtiness and contempt, without authoritarian attitude and
without unbearable paternalism.

Who art in heaven

You are closer to us than we are to ourselves. You come to us, you
speak to us, you make a fellowship with us, and yet we do not
have you at our disposal. We realize that your world has a power
which puts us before a decision.

Hallowed be thy name

We often hear that you are dead. Perhaps a certain name died
and a new name is being born. You lead us to learn to know you
and you do not remain without a name : yet our terms can only
partly and fragmentarily grasp the reality of your existence.

Thy kingdom come

In our hearts we carry a longing for justice, truth, love, freedom,
grace, peace, and joy. These are the signs of your kingdom, but
in our hearts there is also anger, hate, selfishness, and a longing
for revenge. Govern our hearts and the whole of our lives ;
open before us the gate of the land where freedom reigns.

Thy will be done

You cross our paths and do not allow us to think only of ourselves. You want us to live in fellowship with other people. You want us to forget ourselves and live for others.

Give us this day our daily bread

We live in luxury and surplus, although millions of people in this world are hungry. Social inequity, the threat of nuclear war, the cry of children dying of malnutrition and diseases which can be cured — these are the warning signs of our times. We hear your urgent question, "What will you do ?"

And forgive us our trespasses

We often wonder about our hardheartedness ; we are inconsiderate and are not in a position to value the gifts we receive in life. In moments which like lightning illuminate our road, we realize the dangers of our insensitivity and superficiality.

As we forgive them that trespass against us

We think that the weak should forgive and forget. You teach us to understand that forgiveness can be an expression of strength and sovereignty. You judge us by the presence of your love. In its light we learn that, without forgiveness, we would perish in this world.

And lead us not into temptation

We long for power, glory, and property. We do not understand ourselves. We overestimate our strength. We blindly follow doubtful goals. Teach us to bear the burden of our times and lead us out of our disappointments, depressions, and hopelessness.

But deliver us from evil

A fascination with our strength keeps us from seeing the evil in ourselves and the powers which work in this world and which have their own laws. The meeting with you frees us from our fears and gives us courage to struggle with these ambiguous powers.

For thine is the kingdom

Wherever you reign, the people and nations undergo radical changes. Come and compel us to make a new beginning.

The power

We fear people who have power over other people. We know that power is dangerous. The awareness of your dynamic force helps us to see the limitations of our strength and to know that no regime or government can compete with your power.

And the glory

From your presence in history, we learn to see glory where people normally see only suffering, unnecessary sacrifice, and death.

For ever and ever

You upset our human criteria, you help us to get out of the prison of our self-centeredness. You speak the liberating word. You accompany man on his way through history. You are our real Father, from generation to generation.

Amen.

— M. Opocensky   **93**

channel listing

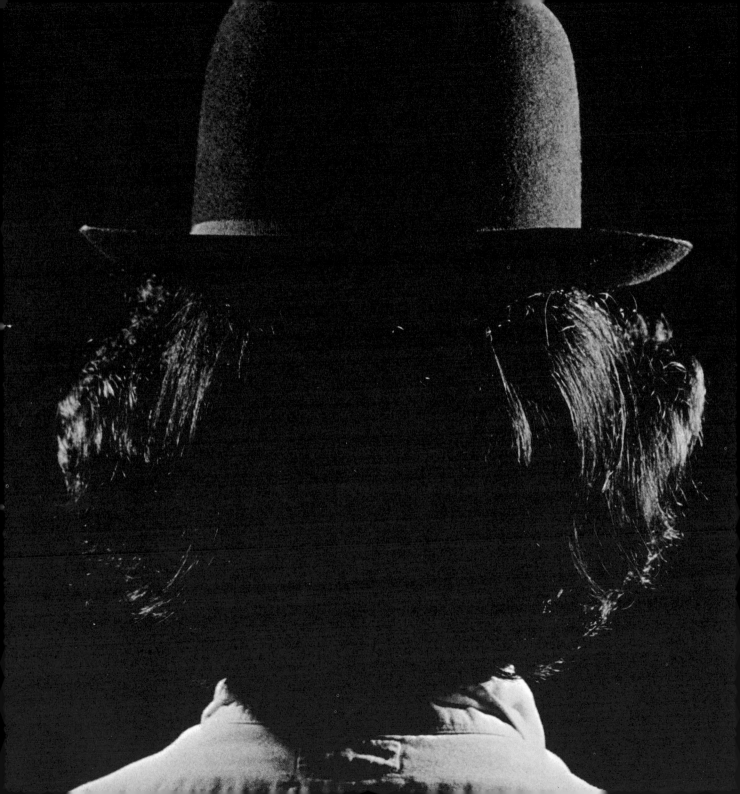